The Tzaddik

and other poems

Per K. Brask

Other FICTIVE PRESS Titles by Per K. Brask

Literary Translations

Foundational Thoughts in Judaism by Andreas Simonsen

The Laws of Life: An Exploration of Fundamental Problems in Ethics by Andreas Simonsen

Poetry Collections

A Spectator: Ekphrastic Poetry

Above Palm Canyon and Other Places in the Mind

Forthcoming

The Foundation of Ethics by Andreas Simonsen

Available in print and e-book formats. To purchase or to learn more about Per K. Brask, visit FictivePress.com

The Tzaddik
and other poems

Per K. Brask

FICTIVE
PRESS

FICTIVE PRESS

First published in 2016 by FICTIVE PRESS, a division of 2815699 Canada Inc., British Columbia, Canada.

Distributed in Canada and worldwide by FICTIVE PRESS.

fictivepress.com

"FICTIVE PRESS" is a trademark of 2815699 Canada Inc.

Cover art: *Toldot* by Janeen Kobrinsky
Cover design: Fictive Press
Author photo: Bonnie Brask

Library and Archives Canada Cataloguing in Publication

Brask, Per K., 1952-

[Poems. Selections]

The tzaddik : and other poems / Per K. Brask. -- First

Fictive Press edition.

Poems.

Issued in print and electronic formats.

ISBN 978-1-927663-43-1 (paperback).--ISBN 978-1-927663-45-5

(epub).--ISBN 978-1-927663-44-8 (mobi).--ISBN 978-1-927663-46-2 (pdf)

I. Title.

PS8553.R296A6 2016   C811'.54   C2016-904645-1

C2016-904646-X

To Rabbi Janeen Kobrinsky of Temple Beth El, Fargo, North Dakota, who shows how pluralism and an unwavering commitment to Judaism can work together.

Introduction

I was not born a Jew. When my wife, Carol Matas, and I got together some forty years ago we quickly became aware that we wanted to make a go of it and that our life together would include children. We decided early on that those children would be raised as Jews—and they have been. That meant that I had a lot of catching up to do and I began to study Judaism.

The more I got into it the more fascinated I became and eventually I fell in love with the conversation Jews have had down through the ages about life and God and what we humans owe to each other and to God. I wanted to join that conversation as a member. We are not a religiously observant family, but we celebrate Shabbat and we are committed to a spiritual Judaism that is eclectically informed by different denominations.

This collection is a result of those years of my living into the world of Judaism.

Per K. Brask

Contents

I HAVE NOT SPOKEN WITH YOU
(for Sam)

I have not spoken with You for so long
I had almost forgotten You
submerged in my inner sea
spinning a vortex of my small desires
until – in a gasp – I remembered
it is Your breath
that sustains the world
Your breath that generates all that is
so none of us is alone
all is connected

despair obliged me to reconnect
or to drown
and for the choice I thank You
and for now knowing that gratitude can keep me afloat
and close to Your hovering breath

EIGHT POEMS FROM KABBALAH

1
THE ORDER OF THE SEFIROT

leads down
and up
funneling
surprise
and desire
to be purified
its downward
flow
is grace
to be taken
up at will
upwards, well
against so much
fiendish ego
defiance
only periodic
passionate battles
invariably
followed by
slipping
embody
the climb
for me
but the beauty
of the tree
beckons
return
return
you are not
alone

2
THE WHITE FIRE
and the black
the settled mind
receiving
the waters
from heaven
by the womb
of creation
the settled mind
attached
to a lattice
of roots
from which no
cuttings
must be taken
the settled mind
understands
the necessary
balances
judgment
mercy
and the beauty
of the world
to be made
more beautiful
as we become one
with the One
as we climb
intuiting this
yearning
for an experience
of bathing
in Your breath
I am still
but an apprentice
this late
in life

still struggling
with unsettled mind
yet refreshed
from what I have
received
hineini!

3
YETZER HARA

left over
from the darkness
before creation
it charges
my mind
and calcifies
my heart
with ego
desires
wants and demands
for me myself
and I need
to discover
the proper charge
to blow
them open
like rocks
and search for
the gem
inside
turn ambition
into service
craving
into gratitude
for the beauty
that gladdens
and so
unclog
the stream
of affections
joining us

4
THERE'S A RIVER
its waters
a remedy
for the soul
it streams
to forever
in both directions
and it waters
the garden
of all creation
you need
do nothing
but make
a slight adjustment
in your view
to receive
its sustenance
and then
you'll want
to do
all that
you can
to show how
we might
live justly
by its banks

5
WHAT SHOULD BE
our reach
for the benefit
of whom
should we
receive
the Shefa
if not
for all
the love
that spins
through
all
and heats
our hearts
enough
to see
that everything
is as it must be
though far from
perfected
and cannot be
by us
alone

6
HOLINESS CLINGS
like oil
to all elements
and levels
of creation
and we
can ingest
the drops
intentionally. Only
strictness
contracts
leaving
no entry
for spirit
only rust
clinging
to the soul
we must
attend plainly
to hints
interpretations
and uncover
secrets
(Peshat
Remets
Derash
Sod
PaRDeS
the orchard
of Paradise)
for life is
for learning
just as Joni Mitchell
said

7
CHOOSE LIFE

choose life You say
to each individually
having put before us
life and death
blessing and curse
three unavoidable
events
the good and the bad
will happen
that's Your promise
and we know
we will make
some of that
happen ourselves
but a life
of love for You
and benevolence to
those we encounter
will make it easier
to survive blessings
that don't last
and to grasp
that curses also
will pass
that is the deal
and it is good

8
THE TZADDIK
is a sign
pointing the way
s/he may not say
concretely
what you must do
but s/he'll tell you
a story
about the ways
of the king
the queen
daughters and sons
and weddings
and if you
understand
you'll get it
if you don't
s/he'll try again
another story
about the marriage
of the upper
and the lower
worlds
the yod
and the lamed
and of joining
yod heh
with vav heh
and then
if only
for a moment
we will be
in awe that
all the worlds
are inter-connected
removing veil upon veil
before going

back into our daily
distractions
yet still yearning
to start all
over again
stumbling
towards
a better life
in all the worlds

ON THE FIRST NIGHT

of Hanukkah
we light one candle
with a candle
and Kai, nearly four
is excited for
there will be
presents
at the end
he knows
to change
the Shabbat blessing
to shel Hanukkah
but what's it
all about?
a temple
is like
a big castle
for God
why?
Kai's favorite
word
and why indeed
but acceptable
a miracle?
for Kai
the unexpected
the unfathomable
happens
every day
several times
even this
story is
completely new
and strange
but not stranger
than his own life

his curiosity
his amazement
is still alive
and this is
the miracle for us
to remember
on this night
so we may
wonder more

RE-IMAGINING MISHLEI SHLOMO
[Proverbs] 8.22-31

Wisdom calls on us to celebrate life
She lay embedded in the Big Bang to overcome
statistical implausibility and to give direction
to awesome evolution and the best way to think of it all
and how to live in gratitude

She is the gift that comes with Being
She was and is always given the task of vibrating
in and out of time under everything and we hear Her
best by attending to each other for the needs
we know we both have

IN THAT MOMENT

in that moment I noticed that angel wings
make a perfect circle when brought together
above their heads (they are not like bird wings at all)

the angel's back a reflecting surface for training
the Shefa, the ever-present divine flow, more finely
toward you when you tune your mind toward the source

IS THERE ANOTHER WAY

is there another way to say
that every intention could give birth
to new life?

so we must play along
with what arises, choose
to become

without knowing the consequences
only that it's natural
that nothing stands still

everything moves all
the time, targets
too

no aim is true, everything
bends, shifts, folds
and unfolds

is there
a fuller way
to say that?

Yes, Deb Margolin said,
"Life is a costume party in which
anyone may come forward
from behind a mask and reveal
themselves as Moshiach."

if only for a moment
I would add

AT THE PORTLAND ZOO

four grandchildren rush about
competing to be first

to insert the plastic key
that unlocks explanations

some exhibits are outfitted too
with renditions of relative experiences

how does a gazelle see
with its eyes so far apart?

how does a python
sense your presence?

can what these animals perceive
be real, called reality

clearly not our reality
but a reality nonetheless

observation makes it so
and it works to sustain itself

if observation congeals
quantum soup into touch

depending on the observer's kind
then some observer must have been present

at the Big Bang for it to happen
for being to become a history

some ~~awareness~~ that includes all observers
and takes delight in the play of relativities

a graceful giver beyond our ken of all that is

WISDOM ROAD
(for Donna and Kat Healy)

the I Ching
told us
follow wisdom road
a yellow path
luminous with aspens
in fall dress
on Montana's high plains
little did we know
wisdom comes
in wind gusts
at 65 miles/hour
stranding us
in Billings
with little choice
but YAM for nourishment
wanting to see
western art, you know
old masters
like Frederick Remington
and Charles Marion Russell
instead we hurtled
into Willem Volkersz'
"Persistent Memories"
of childhood lost
in Amsterdam
166 children
from his school
lost their lives
in KZ camps
before he sat
in their former seats
blond handcrafted
wooden suitcases
each with name and dates
a boy in neon

his suitcase
packed to leave
wooden clogs
some for infants
in a heap
the shaft of a spade
engraved 'guaranteed
lifetime' protrudes
from the mound
rows of wooden benches
reminiscent
of carpentry class
with perfectly placed
stepped-out-of children's shoes
in front
next to a staircase
of stacked cases
a soulbird escaping
its top – later
crashing a Sunday
afternoon tea fundraiser
we meet two of Billings'
few Jews
Kat and Donna
daughter and mother
carrying the spirit
who help us mourn
shiva-like
Volkersz' memories
and we laugh together
for
as the YAM T-shirt says
art matters

BOREDOM

how is boredom
even possible?
how is not
committing
to this moment
doable?
trees do it
they hold
fast
to the ground
constantly
unafraid
of commitment
to this
or any
moment
they dig in
and get out
of it
as much
as there is
only wavering
in the wind
some plants
of course
only stick
to the surface
but stick well
boredom
is sticking
badly
to the moment
and getting
nothing
in return
going nowhere

slowly
thinking about
elsewhere
maybe with sun
and palm trees
a sticking place
for moments
to become
brilliant
get eaten up
like fruit
leaving
sticky hands
and
a commitment
to take
delight

SO YOU MEAN …

– So you mean to say that you talk to God?

– Yes.

– How?

– It's called prayer.

– Yes, I know that, but does God ever answer back?

– No.

– And why do you think that might be?

– Hmmm.

– Ergo?

– I think She got tired of being misunderstood.

– – –

THE LOGIC OF CAPITAL

it's like
an acid
corroding
through layers
souring dignity
raising
rapacity
to a deity
refuting
the divine
in you and me
worshipping
things and paper
we become
things to use
there is
no other
game to play
if you want
holidays
and a pension plan
you'll get
paper cuts and
moral scars
unavoidable
when you are
playing
your part
off the grid
is an illusion
the nets
will find you
or you them
but we can have
small pockets
of relief

on Shabbat
with people
we love and
taste
the sweetness
that
could be
without
it

TWO IMAGES FIGHTING

two images are now fighting in my mind

a few years back I watched through
a taxi cab window a demonstration
against Israel in Copenhagen
Palestinian flags waved above the crowds
and parents, I suppose they were
held up in the air children
wearing mock suicide bomber vests
the next generation of death-bringers

just the other day Marianne sent me a link
to a Danish TV program that I watched on
my computer. A 38-year-old socialist MP
believing Muslim and female took her good friend
the 85-year-old Chief Rabbi on a car ride
to visit the new mosque and the refugee centre
people they both fight and demonstrate for and in the show
you watch friendship demonstrated across generations and faiths

at the end they walk away from us
hand in hand

self and other must surely meet
because without other there's no self

we can walk hand in hand – deferring final words
or wear death vests through our days, martyrs of endings

SHIMON THE TZADDIK USED TO SAY

Shimon the Tzaddik used to say
that the world stands on
Torah, service [to God] and loving-kindness [toward others]

Rabban Shimon ben Gamliel says
that the world is maintained
by law, truth and peace

Today, Varda bat Yosef told me
during our walk, that the world needs
love, creativity and truth

And I want to say
that the greatest of these
is what adds beauty to our world

THE WORK AHEAD

"Artistic content and spiritual communication are, after all, precisely the same thing." W. Benjamin in a letter to G. Scholem, October 22, 1917.

that it all came from God through the creative word
he once saw

later it all came from the class struggle and dialectics
but auras were mixed in

then he made passages speak by strolling
and wondering

always an angel followed him
its back to the future

recording the debris
left behind

one fellow had trouble with his materialism
and the other with his mysticism

he defended himself to the one
saying, "you don't get it, but you may be right"

to the other he said, "you may be right, but maybe
you didn't get it"

mysticism without dirt becomes delusion
materialism without spirit becomes specious

he listened for resonances, thinking
eventually the answer has to become one

rehearsing what the angel taught
that the shards must be put back together

before Moshiach can come

THE MEANING OF LIFE

the meaning of life is
that it is meaningless to say
that life has no meaning

so said Niels Bohr
in a conversation
with Werner Heisenberg

back in 1933 whilst
chaos unleashed itself
from meaning

now we say that
the question is meaningless
it is unanswerable

as Simonsen said
we must ask, does my life
possess the possibility

of becoming meaningful
and to that the answer
is yes by making an effort

for others

IN THE FOYER

in the foyer my eyes fall
on my Israeli sandals
and I am suddenly in the desert
though it's raining out
and the desert I'm in is another
for I've only ever been to Israel
in my mind and the terrain
of that Israel is filled
with prophets, sages and wise women
in sandals, issuing proclamations
of how we've gone wrong
and of how to return
to the way ahead

RABBI SOLOVEITCHIK SAYS

that pain is experienced
by all living things
only humans know
of suffering
and therefore we
crave redemption
which we can have
I think
by replacing being
with saying something
not anything
but something
becoming
just being carries
the pain experienced
by all living things
just by being
but becoming
may one day
move us closer
to each other
so we can better
rail together
against
solitude
and the horrors
of minds too lonely
but Rabbi Soloveitchik
also says
that it is in aloneness
that we cast off
superficiality
and conformity
where we find
singularity
and can become

a renewed member
reaching out
to you
through the agony
of inspired
gesturing

HILLEL GAVE

Hillel gave you permission
to stand up for yourself
but never to sit
while others suffered
and not to wait
for someone else
to step in
he also said
not to do
what we wouldn't have
others doing to us
or to judge a fellow
before we have stood
in his or her
place
kindness, Chesed,
was his way
of building a fence
around the Torah
kindness, Chesed
is the toughest
charge, harder
than following
rules
in a world
where so many things
scream out
seize me
and forget
what you were called
to do, to cultivate
and to keep
for no cheating
is possible
when it comes
to kindness, Chesed

PSALM 16 VERSE 8
(for Carol)

Shiviti Adonai l'negdi tamid
some say, "I have set the Lord
always before me," others
"I set God before me at all times"

but I can do neither one
or the other

but in solitude

with you
I refuse
to be blinded
by setting
an invented image
between us
when really I need to see you
plainly

as the image of the divine

so together we can till
what must be tilled
make what must be made
sing what must be sung

I am happier among those
who say, "I am ever mindful
of the Lord's presence"
for that I can work on
alone and with you
and both shall we
be moved

ACCORDING TO KIERKEGAARD

our ability to do battle with the future
marks our nobility

struggling with the present is easier
than striving with the future

in the present we confront
a tricky event

striving with the future
we confront ourselves

and no one is stronger
than you and me

and our yearning for redemption
for the mess we've made

of all creation

SEPARATION

clouds what's real
but the yearning
is there
endures
sometimes
into delusion
of grandeur
and
a greater
separation
a danger
the drop
isn't the ocean
but can be
dissolved
in it
and then
no longer
a drop
drops
can also
evaporate
and make
clouds
and then
what?
separation
can work
for us
as long
as we
get that
we are
all needed
at the pumps
keeping

our boat
from flooding
allows
no rest
for anyone
and when we
do separation
itself dissolves
and we
begin to see
what's real
in all
humility

DAYS AND NIGHTS

days and nights
words and exclamations
joys and pains
roll into being
shaping the world
anew, each time
a little difference
a variation
some pass on
some pass away
days and nights
words and exclamations
each time, a little
differently, afresh
a variation

a better fit
a repair?

EXPERIENCE

is there experience
before language?
there is something, of course
something wells up
something clenches
something quickens
and the language I use
tells me, when we talk
whether I'm in love
in trouble or lucky
or if I speak Torah
at that moment
whether I'm in awe
about to do wrong
or overwhelmed by
gratitude for being alive
sometimes love and awe
trouble and warning
luck and gratitude
come together
in a seamless experience
of bliss

TRAILS

it is said
that all good trails
lead to the top
of the mountain
some hazardous
some smoother
some scenic
but the long way
around
and a bird's eye
view will testify
to that, but
we must also
say that without wings
by walking you can
only take one trail
at a time, maybe
change over
if you happen
on a crossing
after which you
must follow the new
and the views
it provides
yes, now
with cell phones
we can talk to friends
(depending
on the service)
on other trails
and make
comparisons
while walking on
once at the top
we may see
how everyone

got to the same
place
and why some
got stuck
in dead ends
no mountain
top to be reached
from there

BY WAY OF TANYA

Rabbi Rami Shapiro
teaches that faith
is training, doing
not precepts
we're to commit
and connect
and get on with
it

Torah, Testament
Koran, Sutra and science
all tell us that we need
one another, everything
relates to everything else

you kill me something
in you dies, the part
that made you and now
you're separate
enjoying your power
perhaps, but that
too will pass

and so will you
instead let's celebrate
this brief time
and what each
can contribute
to make all of life
sparkle with awe

at the miracles
that happen everyday
life and love
on an inner city street
and in our wilderness, too

Acknowledgements

"I have not spoken with You" was first published in *Canadian Jewish News*, Literary Supplement, Passover, 2016.

"The Work Ahead" was first published in *Consciousness, Literature and the Arts*, UK, 15:1, 2014.

"Wisdom Road" was first published in *Consciousness, Literature and the Arts*, UK, 16:3, 2015.

"The Logic of Capital" was posted on the CLASS (Centre for the Liberal Arts and Secular Society) website, University of Winnipeg, October 2015.

"Eight Poems from Kabbalah" were written during a Melton course in Mysticism and Kabbalah taught by Rabbi Alan Green of Congregation Shaarey Zedek in Winnipeg, Canada, in the fall of 2015. I am deeply grateful to Rabbi Green for his teaching.

Thank you to the students in my course "Contemporary Jewish Life" in the Department of Religion and Culture at the University of Winnipeg in the winter term of 2016.

And last but certainly not least I owe a huge thank you to Morri Mostow of Fictive Press.

About Per K. Brask

Per K. Brask is an accomplished poet, dramaturge and author. He has published poetry, plays, short stories, essays and literary translations. His co-translation with Patrick Friesen of Ulrikka S. Gernes' *Frayed Opus for Strings & Wind Instruments* was short listed for the 2016 Griffin Poetry Prize. Per is a Professor in the Department of Theatre and Film at the University of Winnipeg. He lives in Winnipeg, Canada, with his wife, Carol Matas, an international bestselling author of books for young people.

For a more complete biography, visit: fictivepress.com/per-brask.htm.

www.ingramcontent.com/pod-product-compliance
Lightning Source LLC
Chambersburg PA
CBHW031226090426
42740CB00007B/727